Kellie Beckmann-Quin

Stuff the Status Quo

*Spend less on keeping a roof over your head
& more on living a life you love*

Copyright © 2024 by Kellie Beckmann-Quin

All rights reserved. No part of this publication may be reproduced, stored or transmitted in any form or by any means, electronic, mechanical, photocopying, recording, scanning, or otherwise without written permission from the publisher. It is illegal to copy this book, post it to a website, or distribute it by any other means without permission.

Exceptions permitted by The Copyright Act 1968 include: reviewers who may quote brief passages in a review; journalists who may reference the book in an article or news report; and house sitters who may use the "House Sitters Checklist" when booking their own personal sits.

First edition

ISBN: 9781763596610

This book was professionally typeset on Reedsy.
Find out more at reedsy.com

Contents

I   Part One

1   Live with no Regrets   3
    The time and money trap   3
    Status quo   4
2   WHY would YOU live rent-free?   7
    Choices   9
    Do the right thing   10

II Part Two

3   WHO can live rent-free?   15
    Can I really do this?   16
4   WHEN is the best time to live rent-free?   22
    Short-term strategies: Save for a big purchase or
    pay off debt   23
    Making it Permanent   28
5   WHERE can you live rent-free?   30
    Local - Going rent-free in your own backyard   30
    Border crossing - interstate or international   37
    Bright city lights   38
    Rural retreat   38
    Exotic and unique locations   39
    Woop-woop: remote locations   41

6	What about WORK?	46
	Work remotely	47
	Portable work	47
	Locums	47
	Seasonal work	48

III Part Three

7	HOW to live rent-free with the Alt Accom lifestyle	53
	House sitting	54
	What exactly does a house sitter do?	54
	Where to find house sits	57
	Why register on a paid site	59
	Set up your sitter profile	62
	How to apply for a sit	64
	RV or vanlife	67
	Gone Wheelabout – tales from the road	67
	Choosing the right RV for you	71
	Property caretaking	73
	What is caretaking?	73
	How to find a gig	75
	Exchange Volunteering	77
	Where to find exchange opportunities	78
	Job that includes accommodation	79
	All aboard - floating homes	80
	Artist in residence - for creatives	81
8	QUIZ: Find your best fit	83

IV Part Four

9	RESOURCES - From dreaming to doing	89
	Action sheets	89
	First steps	90
10	Letting stuff go – how to declutter and simplify	94
	Mail sorted	96
11	RV Quiz	98
12	House Sitter Checklist	101
13	Reader bonuses	107
	Discount code	107
	Community	108

Acknowledgement   109
About the Author   110

I

Part One

1

Live with no Regrets

In November 2009, Australian palliative care worker Bronnie Ware blogged about regrets that dying patients shared with her. The massive global response to that post led to her writing a book, *The Top Five Regrets of the Dying*. The number one regret was this:

> **"I wish I'd had the courage to live a life true to myself, not the life others expected of me."**

What is it about death that forces us to face our fears? Why can't we summon the courage to live our own authentic life, until the threat of losing it is staring us in the face?

The time and money trap

Four years after Bronnie published her book about regrets of the dying, I experienced a death. The death of my marriage literally meant the end of one life and the beginning of another. I went from married with a mortgage, to single in a share-house.

Two unsuccessful share-houses later, I finally gave in and got my own rental lease. A tiny one-bedroom unit. The rent and utility bills took a major part of my income.

I had plans, goals, dreams. I wanted to travel, write a book, work less, live more. My new full-time job in the city paid okay, but keeping a roof over my head was making it hard to get ahead. My largest expense in life was keeping me stuck where I was. Two years later I'd had enough.

During after work drinks, I shared my frustration with a friend. She nodded sympathetically, "It's what we have to do though isn't it. All part of being a productive member of society." Exasperated, I banged my drink down on the table, "Who makes these rules? I don't want to follow them anymore. Stuff the status quo!"

Status quo

What is the status quo? In this case, it's whatever the conventional, traditional, or prevailing social attitudes are, in regard to where you call home. According to mainstream western cultures, renting or buying real estate is the normal way to keep a roof over your head.

What is normal? In this instance, it's a state of being or living considered standard or common within a specific group. But here's the catch. Normality is relative to who or what you're comparing something with. Who we hang out with, in a community sense of the word, shapes our view of what is "normal". If we hang out with people who spend most of their income on paying rent or a mortgage, the status quo has become that.

Essential needs versus cultural expectations

The basic essentials for humans to live well, according to Maslow's Hierarchy of Needs, is food, water and shelter. What do most people spend the majority of their income on? The largest ongoing life expense is shelter. Keeping a roof overhead. Paying rent or a mortgage, along with utility bills, maintenance and more. For some crazy reason, people accept this as a normal essential cost of life.

Maslow's theory assumes everyone values specific needs at the same level. The hierarchy of needs doesn't allow for diversity. It ignores personal or cultural differences. When we add a layer of social and cultural expectations to how we 'should' keep a roof over our head, we get the stereotype of tenant or mortgage owner.

Living rent-free in alternative accommodation (Alt Accom) is a counter-cultural method of reducing living costs, so you can free up time/money for **what really matters to you**. What you do with the extra time/money is totally your choice. Having those kind of choices equals freedom.

Still, it takes bravery to say, "Stuff the status quo!" and then make life choices based on our own priorities. Counter-cultural choices that go against the flow, are the domain of the courageous.

Even in the current socio-political environment of diversity and inclusion, we still fear being different. It begs the question, why are we so afraid to live life on our own terms?

Cultural conditioning

One of our greatest psychological needs, is the need to belong. To be part of a group, we need to fit in. From the wide-angle lens of fitting in with society, to the narrower focus of fitting in with family and friends, it matters to us.

We fear other people's opinions. We fear their judgement, disapproval, or derision if we don't follow 'the script' or meet their expectations.

Script?

Yeah, you know, those unwritten rules like:

"A successful responsible adult sets up a home and works hard all their life to pay the rent or mortgage to keep a roof over their head."

This keeping a roof over our head consumes the largest part of our income. Maintaining it consumes a large part of our time. Most people, like my friend, shrug and say, "What else can we do?" We base our financial and life decisions on mainstream models of success because we fear being different.

The big woolly mammoth of cultural conditioning is a huge beast. It takes courage to go up against it. What would you rather do; live a life of quiet desperation keeping up appearances, or live a life of freedom from the status quo, spending your time and money on what matters to you, not others?

Thankfully, since the day I said, "Stuff the status quo!" I made changes that allowed me to enjoy several years of living rent-free. I've been able to work less, live more, save more and tick off some cool life goals.

It's not too good to be true. It is totally achievable for you too!

When you know your WHY, I can show you HOW.

2

WHY would YOU live rent-free?

I f someone told me ten years ago that I'd be living in my favourite part of Australia, writing a book, I would have laughed. Back then I was writing stuff for other people, working 9-5 and spending big chunks of my income just to keep a roof over my head.

Today, as I write this book, I'm sitting in a house on a hill, looking out over a forest. If that's not special enough, I'm living rent-free and pay no utility bills. As an extra bonus, if it's a sunny day, I can head up the road for a walk on some spectacular beaches. That's what I call living the dream.

Your dream is probably different. Maybe your passion is cycling, world travel or starting your own business.

1. While writing this book, I lived rent-free as caretaker of this property.

Living rent-free gives you choices. You can:

- work less and live more
- work the same and save more
- travel on a tiny budget
- gain a qualification
- save to buy your own home
- [-insert your dream here-]

You can choose the rent-free lifestyle forever, or for a short time, to free up finances for something other than keeping a roof over your head.

Have you noticed a word that keeps popping up? Choose.

Choices

Recently someone said to me they had no choices where they were at. Sure, sometimes it feels like that. Life throws hurdles in our way. Sometimes, we even block ourselves. But we always have choice. Even if it means choosing our own mindset. We can choose to turn our back on victim mentality and embrace a mindset of resilience and resourcefulness.

So why would YOU choose to live rent-free? Maybe you're like me and you want to write a book, but you don't have enough time. You're so busy working just to keep a roof overhead, there's no energy left at the end of the day. When stuck on the hamster wheel of go-go-go, your creative mojo becomes a nojo.

If you could gain freedom from rent or mortgage, what **dreams** would <u>you</u> chase?

Do you want to break free?

Are you like I was, sick of being stuck in the time and money trap? Are you working hard just to keep a roof over your head? I'm going to share hard-earned wisdom and experience that can help you break free and find the courage to live life on your own terms. In this book, I will teach you about Alt Accom options, whether you live in the city or country, pros and cons, digital resources and more.

Here's what you need to do FIRST

1. Work out how much you spend on keeping a roof over your head. Rent or mortgage payments, utility bills, maintenance costs – gardening, mowing, washing windows, painting. Include all of it. Even tools you need to own like lawnmower, ladders, or vacuum cleaner. Write that

figure down. Then work out what percent of your income that is and write that figure down.

2. Imagine if you no longer had those costs and responsibilities. If you had the courage to live a life true to yourself, not the life others expect of you, what would you do with the extra time and money? You might have one main goal, or a few. Write down what choices you'd make.

Your answers offer insight into what you *really* value in life. These stepping-stones can lead you down the path to a life lived on your own terms. A life aligned with your own values.

Do the right thing

Have you noticed when something seems too good to be true, we often wonder, "Is that even legal?" When talking about my rent-free lifestyle to others, I've noticed a recurring theme in their questions. The words used and the questions asked are all different, but mostly they boil down to one thing. Is living rent-free:

- **ethical** – shaped by principles of right and wrong
- **legal** – related to rules and regulations, or
- **moral** – aligned with personal beliefs and values?

The answer? A resounding YES! Many forms of Alt Accom feature a win-win service-based element. When considering ethics, any choice that involves helping other people has to be a good one.

There may be rules and regulations around a certain type of Alt Accom, but they vary a lot depending on your location. A key part of your planning should include research to consider any legal requirements that might apply to your situation.

When we make choices that align with our personal beliefs and values, we are choosing to live with integrity. One of my core values is to intentionally build a simple life that embraces minimalism. The way I choose Alt Accom allows me to walk that talk. It's not a necessary part of the rent-free lifestyle, but it's one positive I've embraced.

Freedom to choose

Mainstream ways of keeping a roof overhead can force us to do things that don't align with our core beliefs and values. The first step towards personal freedom involves having choice. My hope, in writing this book, is to offer alternatives for you to consider. What you do with this information is your choice.

Mindset over money

Sure, at first my **'why'** was to cut the cost of keeping a roof overhead. Apart from the obvious financial wins, however, one of the reasons I continue to enjoy this lifestyle is the connection and service elements. Yep, this is one of the best kept secrets about living rent-free.

Most Alt Accom options have an inbuilt service element. Wherever I'm living, it's because I'm helping someone. That's my mindset and it gives me purpose. Generally, it's a simple transactional exchange. Service with a smile is all part of this win-win lifestyle.

So, how has Alt Accom allowed me to help people?

House sitting

I help people travel for work or leisure. By taking care of their home, pets and plants, I help owners relax while they are away.

Property caretaking

I help people manage their properties. By tending gardens, livestock, fences, or B&B's, I help owners maintain peace of mind in their absence, knowing their farm or retreat is cared for.

WWOOFING (World Wide Opportunities on Organic Farms)

I help people with projects on their farm or homestead. By planting crops, rescuing injured sheep, or cooking up a meal or preserves from freshly picked produce, I provide an extra pair of hands onsite. In exchange, they provide me food and board.

Volunteering

I help people with my professional expertise by creating social media content, marketing or other business writing. I help farm stays, charities or business owners, tell their story better.

Sometimes, when the concept of rent-free living is raised, the perception might be it's for freeloaders. My experience puts that concept to rest. If you're a helper, like to have meaning and purpose in life beyond the status quo stuff, then Alt Accom options are your ticket to the whole world.

II

Part Two

3

WHO can live rent-free?

After eight years of choosing Alt Accom options, rent-free living is normal for me. Boy was I in for a surprise when doing market research for this book! I was shocked and amused to discover what some people think living rent-free is all about.

What it's NOT - hobos, squatters, sex workers or freeloaders!

When I asked potential readers what questions they had about living rent-free, this is what some of them said:

> *I'd love to save my rent money, but I don't want to be a homeless hobo.*
> *Squatting is illegal and you should stop sponging off other people.*
> *Is this one of those 'sex for rent' arrangements?*
> *How do you find a sugar mummy or daddy?*

While rent-free living does go against the status quo, I can assure you, it's all legal, nothing to do with sex work and is a lifestyle choice made by a diverse range of people. Regardless of your personal profile or stage of life, you can live rent-free.

Can I really do this?

Are you wondering if Alt Accom options are suitable for your situation? The best thing about this lifestyle is the diversity of people engaging and benefiting from it.

Young adults – footloose and fancy free!

If you're just starting out in life, you probably want to spread your wings, explore the world and gain independence. If you want to travel, then rent-free living will work for you. Options like vanlife, volunteering or finding a job that provides accommodation might appeal to you.

Got wheels and want to travel? Maybe vanlife is for you. Instead of paying rent to stay in one place, you can set up a vehicle as your roof overhead and travel for seasonal jobs where accommodation, or a site to park up with power and water, is part of your package.

If vanlife isn't your jam, keep reading for hints and tips on how to choose the best rent-free option for your situation.

Fresh graduates - entry level income but want boss level lifestyle?

If you've just left college or university and scored the first gig in your new career, setting up a home base can cost a fortune. Think about it. You'll need to pay for:

- a deposit to secure a rental lease
- furnishing an entire house/apartment
- tools for kitchen, garden and garage
- utility connections and bills.

It's hard to get excited about a new career and your income earning potential, when establishing a roof over your head gobbles up the first 6-12 months of your pay.

Why not choose a rent-free option and live in a comfortable home, sometimes with extras like a pool, home theatre, gym and some fun pets to play with. House sitting gives you all that and more. Simply bring your bag, experience with animals/gardens and you're all set to enjoy that boss level lifestyle without the price tag.

Wannabe home owners

If you want to save for a house deposit - this will get you there! Sick of being a tenant and want to buy your own home? There's three basic ways you can build a nest egg:

- earn more
- spend less
- save more.

If you choose to live rent-free for a while, you may not earn more, but you will cut the largest living expense from your budget. You'll spend a lot less and save a lot more. So, in reality, it's a roundabout way to earn more.

Imagine cutting your rent out of the budget. How much money would that save you each week or month? How many months till you could save a house deposit?

If you're a creative, an Artist-in-residence program could provide rent-free accommodation while you work on your book, photography, art, music and so on. House sitting is another housing option with no cost to you other than watering plants and feeding pets.

Families with dependent kids

Those of you in the child-rearing stage might think this lifestyle is not for you. Sure, you need to consider education, childcare, playgroups, daily routine and all the things parents need to make decisions about. It all comes back to your "why".

Maybe you want to work less so you can spend more time with your kids while they're young. If childcare costs as much as you're earning, how can you get ahead to save for your own home, a holiday or pay off debt?

Perhaps your kids are early teens, and you want to make family memories together before they leave the nest. Digital nomad choices are booming. The internet makes finding seasonal or locum work easier. Many families are travelling the country or the world, together. Their kids are gaining real world experiences that enhance traditional education.

For those wanting to stay in one place for traditional schooling, RV lifestyle or house sitting options are being adopted by families with kids of all ages. A quick search online will connect you with parents just like you who have chosen alternative accommodation to reduce living costs and free up time and money for quality experiences together as a family.

Midlife mavericks - craving more, or less, at the halfway point

Are you somewhere between 40 and 50 years old? If you're middle-aged, you may be reflecting on where you've been and what you've done with your life. You might be asking yourself questions like:

- Is that all there is?
- Does my life have meaning?
- Have I made the right choices?

The answers to those questions might cause you to re-evaluate priorities and lifestyle choices. Your kids may have left home, you might want to downsize your expenses, but upsize your living.

You might be due long-service-leave from work. House sitting is a rent-free way of travelling, broadening your horizons and giving you space to mentally process changes you might want to make for the second half of your life.

If house sitting doesn't grab you, but you'd like to explore Alt Accom as a short- or long-term option while you reassess life goals, keep reading. There's much more here for you.

Silver nomads - Retirees on minimal pensions, or homeowners wanting to roam

Getting older has its perks. Usually, it means retirement from the daily grind of full-time work. Many of us look forward to that stage of life. That time when we have freedom to do what we want, when we want, where we want.

Being free from a workplace routine opens up many Alt Accom options. You may like to get an RV and hit the road for an extended amount of time. Perhaps you'd like to learn new ways of gardening as a volunteer on an organic farm, where you're provided meals and accommodation in exchange for your help. If you love ocean sailing, doing yacht relocations might be the right choice.

Now your income has stopped, if you're renting, or still have a mortgage, you may feel stuck and not able to travel or experience adventures like the ones above. If you sublease or rent your current home out to tenants (maybe family or friends), that in effect gives you a rent-free lifestyle no matter which option you choose. You'll find more detail about how you can do this in the HOW section.

Diversity list – my personal profile

Even my own experience shows how flexible this way of living can be. This snapshot of my profile gives you an idea of just how diverse and inclusive the rent-free lifestyle can be:

Work status: I've lived rent-free while working full time in an office, full time remotely, part-time remotely and in holiday mode.

Nationality and ethnicity: I was born in Australia as a fourth generation Australian. My ancestors were from Scotland, Ireland, England and Prussia/Germany. While most of my rent-free living has been in Australia, I've also lived rent-free internationally. I know people of many nationalities and ethnic identities who live rent-free too.

Age: I started the rent-free lifestyle in my 40's, although I did stints of it in my late teens, early twenties, and thirties. Yep, I didn't realise it at the time, but my first foray into rent-free living happened as a teenager. I moved to the city and took a job as a live-in nanny. I wasn't sure what direction I wanted to go in career-wise, but this move gave me a roof over my head, an income and time to decide what vocational study I really wanted to do. Since then, I've got to know people of all ages who live rent-free by choosing Alt Accom options.

Gender and sexuality: I'm a heterosexual female, but I know people from a wide range of gender identities and sexual orientations who live rent-free.

Health status: I've lived rent-free as a reasonably fit and healthy person. I also have an invisible disease, so most people are unaware of it. Some days I feel physically great and other days I need to rest. I've got to know others with chronic illness or a disability, and caregivers whose partner/child needs care, who successfully live rent-free. They, like me, enjoy the reduced need to work just to keep a roof overhead.

Relationship status: I've lived rent-free as a single, as part of a couple, and with 3 kids in tow. There are families, couples and singles who use

Alt Accom as their preferred lifestyle choice. Some for a short time, others all the time.

The truth is there's an Alt Accom option to suit 96 percent of people. Two percent will have legitimate reasons they cannot live rent-free. The other two percent simply don't want to consider an alternative and are happy with the status quo.

Alt Accom options free up the money you would normally spend on rent or your mortgage.

1. Which stage of life are you in?
2. What would you do with the extra time or money that rent-free living can give you?

4

WHEN is the best time to live rent-free?

The folk-rock hit sung by The Byrds in the sixties says it all. "To everything there is a season." This timeless lyric was actually taken from Ecclesiastes in the Bible, written in the 10th century. Here we are in the 21st century and that wisdom still applies.

We've already talked about life *stages*. As the second half of that word suggests, they are mostly linked with age. Seasons of life may not be linked directly with age.

Maybe it helps to think of seasons as chapters. Everyone's story is unique, and the chapters may happen in a different order. Here's what I mean. Think about three things that could happen at any age. Off the top of my head, here's three things; divorce, death and a dog. Someone could get a divorce, get a terminal diagnosis or get a dog in their 20's, 30's, 40's, 50's . . . got it?

Speaking from experience, divorce is a messy chaotic chapter or season in anyone's life. My experiment with Alt Accom options started then. I was trying to maintain a lifestyle on a single income. It was a never-ending cycle of work-bills-work. Divorce was an ending that led me to consider a new beginning in how I kept a roof over my head.

If you've just had a terminal diagnosis or lost your partner to a terminal disease or accident, you'll make different choices about how and where you live. What one person chooses in those circumstances might not be the same choice another makes. For some, this might be a season where self-care is more important than working. Living rent-free can take the financial pressure off.

For others, a trip to places they've always wanted to see, becomes more important than staying home, mowing lawns and washing windows. Living rent-free with Alt Accom options, offers an affordable way to tick the bucket-list off.

Getting a puppy or rescue dog is another season that can happen any time in your life. When you're training a dog to pee and poo outside, that's probably not the best time to consider house sitting. If you want to consider rent-free living in that chapter, the RV vanlife option or property caretaking might be more suitable.

Short-term strategies: Save for a big purchase or pay off debt

Living rent-free can be your ticket to achieving financial goals or dreams. If you want to save for a big ticket-item, pay off debt, or go on a round-the-world trip, Alt Accom options are a great short-term strategy.

Ditch your debt

Are you like me and want to live debt free? Debt is like a heavy anchor on a chain. It weighs us down. Debt creates a never-ending cycle of, "I owe, I owe, it's off to work I go." Debt keeps us in jobs we dislike and places where we feel stuck.

If your bank account is in the red, showing more minuses than plusses, living rent-free or with zero mortgage, can help you pay off debt and start saving.

Instead of paying your rent or mortgage each week or month, choose an Alt Accom option. This will free up your money and let you pay your debt off. Fast! You'll be amazed how much freedom there is when every cent you earn goes into current and future expenditures, not past ones.

Savings calculator

Here's a little exercise for you. Get a pen and write this down:
   What are you saving for?
   How much do you need?
   How much do you spend on rent/mortgage each week/month?
   If you funnelled rent/mortgage payments into savings instead, how many weeks/months would it take you to save what you need?
   Most people are amazed how fast and how much they can save when they cut the cost of keeping a roof overhead. You may have your own home or a rental that you love and are happy with. That doesn't mean you can't live rent-free for a short time.

The savings savvy subletter or homeowner

If you want to live rent-free for a short time but have an already established home, you can rent out or sublet your home fully furnished.*
Sometimes this is called a turnkey lease or rental. Not only does this help you save your rent/mortgage money, it also saves you paying storage fees for furniture.

Who will rent your furnished home?

Typically, tenants who rent furnished properties are looking for a temporary place to live, until they return home elsewhere or find a more permanent place to call home. Tenants who look for fully furnished/turnkey rental homes include:

Relocation or corporate executives

Relocation rentals are for people moving regionally, interstate or across international borders for work purposes. These renters need a place to live when first relocating for a new job. Often an organisation finds and pays for relocation accommodation for their employee.

Travelling professionals

Some examples of this kind of short-term tenant include:
- A medical professional who works locums to cover the absence of a local health practitioner.
- Long distance commuters have a secondary place of residence close to their workplace. Common terms for this include: FIFO (fly-in fly-out), DIDO (drive-in drive-out) or BIBO (bus-in bus-out).
- Project staff working on contract for a specific job that ends when the project is complete. The type of projects might include establishing infrastructure like roads, construction or technology.

New arrivals

Not everyone who moves to a new place is relocating for work. Other people who rent furnished properties include:
- students
- recent graduates
- divorced or separated
- long-stay tourists.

These type of tenants seek fully furnished accommodation because they want a relaxed transition into their new stage of life. They want a 'home-away-from-home' experience with all the comforts they would have in their own home.

Save on storage fees

Instead of paying to store your furniture, linens, towels, kitchen appliances and more, you can earn money by renting your home with all those items included. Depending on your location and type of property, you can charge 15 to 50 percent more rent for a fully furnished property. *

Caveats

Legalities - Short-term rentals are usually up to one month. You need to be aware that short-term rentals usually have more legislation around them now, due to the boom in Air BnB and similar platforms. Medium term rentals are more than one month, but less than 12 months, and can be easier to navigate from a legal point of view. Long term rentals are more than one year in length *

Insurance – If you rent your home out through AirBnB, they provide some level of insurance for your property. You need to establish whether that insurance will cover your needs, or if you need to take out a separate landlord insurance. *

Confessions from a former tenant - How I sublet my apartment and tasted freedom

When I first decided to try RV life as an Alt Accom option, I kept a safety net. I'd already established a comfortable home in a great location. Close to public transport for commuting to work, a beach for the backyard, great cafes in walking distance and a small shopping centre nearby. If I was going to stay in the city, this was where I wanted to be.

However, a recent RV purchase meant I was keen to hit the road and see if a nomadic lifestyle would work for me. I couldn't afford to take a month off work to travel and also keep paying rent. So, I got creative and sublet my fully furnished apartment to free me up for a road trip. The couple who moved into my apartment were a corporate relocation. She was sponsored to Australia from the UK by her employer. They covered a short relocation rental to allow her time to find her own place.

2. My first campervan and motorhome parked out the front of my Sydney apartment building. Subletting the apartment let me upgrade and hit the road on an extended trip that turned into a full-time nomad lifestyle.

When I wanted to extend my RV accommodation adventure, she decided to extend the sublease with me herself, for the convenience of a fully set up home in a great location by the beach. The following year, she took over my lease officially and bought my entire house lot of furniture, appliances and linens. Selling it all in one go saved me so much time and mucking around, I gave it to her for a very good price. Buying the house-lot saved her hours of shopping, physical effort to move large items up two flights of stairs and assembling furniture. I was happy, she was happy. It was a win for both of us.

Even if you have an established home, you can still choose to live rent- or mortgage-free for a short time. Hold your goal in front of you. Do you want to save for a big ticket-item, pay off debt, go on a round-the-world trip or something else? Alt Accom options allow you to have your cake and eat it too. All it takes is some creative thinking and a willingness to move outside the status quo.

* *Gain professional advice from your financial advisor or accountant about any legal or tax implications of renting out or subletting your home.*

Making it Permanent

Full-time travellers or those rethinking what really matters in life

You might decide, like I did, that Alt Accom options are your ticket to freedom. After a taste of the lifestyle, I wanted to make it an ongoing way of keeping a roof over my head. I closed the chapter on my apartment life in Sydney and went full-time nomad.

How did I do it?

Over the next eight years, I created a combination of rent-free living options that worked perfectly for me. I travelled Australia and overseas

at very low cost in the following ways:
1. RV life
2. House sitting
3. Property caretaking
4. Volunteerism, and
5. Exchange.

What works for you may be different. The important thing is to consider which ones might be your best option.

See the **First Steps** action sheet at the end of this book to help determine what your Alt Accom starter style is, and which type best suits your situation.

5

WHERE can you live rent-free?

Regardless of where you live, or where you would like to live, chances are there's an Alt Accom option in that area. From city apartments to outback paddocks, and everywhere in between, the locations you can live rent-free are only limited by your imagination. If you can think outside the square, you can live there.

Local - Going rent free in your own backyard

Do you like the idea of living rent-free, but want to stay in the same area? There are many reasons why you might need to stay local. Circumstances that tie you to a specific place include:

- **work** that requires onsite attendance
- **study** on campus at school, college or university
- **family** support for aging parents, grandkids or your kids
- **commitments** with a sports club, church or community group
- **health** issues needing access to medical care or weather that benefits the condition.

Non-home owners

Maybe you don't have an existing home-base but want to stay in one area, consider local house sitting. People need their pets, plants or garden looked after. They may be travelling for work, leisure, a wedding, medical care or study.

Obviously, you'll find more house sits in a large city, but even in smaller towns, it's surprising how many people need a. The key is to let people know what you're doing. I spent one year house sitting in a smaller town and once the word got out, I had more requests than I had time for.

In a country town you will find an interesting mix of houses, animals and gardens that need someone to care for them while the owner is away.

From cute country cottages to large sprawling farms, from pets to livestock, from little lap dogs to working farm dogs, and from pot-plants to permaculture gardens, I've lived rent-free as a result of helping others travel when they need to. You can too! Once you start looking for those opportunities, you'll be amazed how many there are and how good it is to find such a win-win solution for all parties involved.

If you're serious about living rent-free, house sitting can work as a short- or long-term strategy. Scattered through this book, and in the chapter on house sitting, you'll find many more hints, tips and insider info on this option.

Homeowners

If you're a home or property owner and have the space, you can literally go rent-free in your own backyard. Why not create a self-contained living area. Depending on your needs, you could move out of the main house and rent that out or stay in the main house and rent the smaller space.[*]

House hacking is a specific strategy where the property owner shares their space with tenants. It might be a bedroom and shared bathroom/kitchen or a shed for storage in the back yard. The income earned goes toward covering the property owner's mortgage payments.

With part, or all, of your mortgage being covered by an onsite tenant, you give yourself choice. Maybe you want to work part-time instead of full-time or continue working as you are and save money for an upcoming event or purchase. When you have choices, you have more freedom.

To give examples of different ways to live rent-free in your own backyard, let me share a few stories. They might inspire you with practical ideas on how to gain freedom from being stuck in the status quo of paying a mortgage or rent.

Build or install a studio/granny flat

When I was married, we decided to become owner-builders and designed and built a house. We had a mortgage on the property and didn't want to also pay rent for a house in town while we were building.

As part of the overall property development, we built a shouse (shed house). A huge 4-bay shed was divided in half. Two bays were the shed proper with tools, vehicles and stuff that gets stored in sheds. The other two bays were walled, lined, had a sealed floor, windows, doors, a kitchen and bathroom. An open living area included a bedroom behind a curtained-off corner.

Building the actual house took us three years as we both worked full time. Living onsite in the shouse saved us about $54,000 in rent elsewhere. It cost a lot less than that to set up. Once the actual house was complete, the shouse became a studio space and rustic self-contained guesthouse.

3. Rather than rent a house offsite while owner-building, living onsite in half a shed fit out as a temporary house, saved more than $50,000 in rent.

These days there are multiple options on the market for prebuilt modular studios, granny flats or tiny homes. So, if you're not a builder, you can still choose this option.* Of course, the initial outlay may be more, but if you work out the cost versus savings or earnings long term, it could be a good investment.

Imagine living rent- or mortgage-free in your own backyard. Whether you're already a property owner or a non-homeowner, it is possible for you to live rent-free in your local area, even literally your own backyard.

Set up an RV onsite

Here's another idea to consider. Do you have an RV that only gets used a couple of times a year? You could put this to good use as a way to reduce the cost of your own accommodation.

If you live near a popular tourist destination, university, hospital, or agricultural farms, providing seasonal accommodation for workers can be a great way to generate income towards the costs of keeping a roof over your own head. There are a few ways you could use an RV onsite to achieve this.

Short term downsizing for long term gain

Sally lives on a waterfront property and owns an RV. During peak holiday periods, she rents her house to families on vacation. She packs personal and important items into a locked storage area, then moves herself out to the RV. It's self-contained and located in a separate part of the property. She has privacy and so do her holiday tenants. Sally earns enough money from the holiday rentals to cover the small mortgage remaining on her property.

4. An unused backyard RV could offset your own rent or mortgage.

Smart savings

Tye and Leah live in a university town. Each semester they rent their RV out to a student. The money they make on that covers 35 percent of their own rent.

Healthy outlook

Lisa lives near a hospital. Many of the medical staff there are rostered on alternating weeks. They often live too far away to commute every day, so she rents out her RV in the backyard. The money she earns doing that, has allowed her to quit work and write romance novels.

Harvesting good returns

Jane and Mike live in a rural town and put their RV to good use when nearby farms are harvesting. Seasonal workers rent their RV as accommodation. The extra income allowed Jane to cut back to part-time work. She now spends one day a week working on her landscape paintings, in preparation for her annual art exhibition.

Convert an existing shed

Maybe you don't have the budget to build a brand-new studio or granny flat on your property. Do you have an existing shed or outbuilding that could be converted to studio style accommodation?

During the early months of the pandemic, I escaped the east coast of Australia with my partner at the time, to the less populated state of South Australia. We were full-time nomads with an enjoyable lifestyle exploring the country on road trips with an RV and helping others by house sitting. Travel restrictions during the pandemic put an immediate stop to our usual way of life.

Seeking an alternative to crowded caravan parks for an unknown period of time, we decided to buy a block of land. This was before the pandemic had a chance to profoundly impact the economy, including massive real estate price jumps.

Specific requirements included an existing shed, septic tank, and room to grow fruit and vegetables. We found a bargain in a tiny hamlet, 10 minutes from a coastal village and 45 minutes from a large town.

The block was perfect. We insulated, lined and fit-out half the existing shed with cooking facilities, kitchen cupboards, wardrobe and sofa bed. A washing machine was integrated into the old outhouse. I planted fruit and vegetables to supplement the existing fruit trees.

The block of land was so cheap, we paid cash for it from a small savings account. Instead of being thousands of dollars out of pocket paying rent or site fees at a caravan park, the block allowed rent- and mortgage-free living during the pandemic.

The timing and your circumstances will be different. If you already own property and want to minimise or cover your mortgage payments, think about how you could convert or re-purpose an existing shed or outbuilding.*

Your ticket to rent- or mortgage-free living might be in your own backyard. Consider upgrading existing structures or an RV as an additional onsite accommodation option.

Get informed about local property laws and seek advice from your financial advisor on implications of renting part or all of your home.

Border crossing - interstate or international

In *The Merry Wives of Windsor*, Shakespeare wrote about the world being our oyster. When it comes to Alt Accom, this is my favourite catchcry. The world really is your oyster when looking for a rent-free roof overhead.

Whether you're temporarily visiting or permanently moving across borders, you can find rent-free options in most places. You'll save thousands of dollars on standard hotel, B&B or rentals. When you live like a local, your experience will also be more authentic. Instead of staying in the tourist bubble with premium prices, you can stay longer, get involved in the community and make genuine connections with local people.

Bright city lights

Do bright city lights flip your switch? Then you'll be pleased to know there's many Alt Accom options in high density living regions. From downtown city skyscrapers to suburban homes, there's a place you can live rent-free.

Large cities are called "the big smoke" in many countries. This colloquial term originated in the 1800s and refers to the smoky haze created by large populations living and working in a relatively small area. The more population and industry there is in a city, the more opportunities you will find for rent-free living.

Just like I've done in the past, you might keep a roof over your head by securing a:

- job with onsite accommodation
- city or suburban house sit
- or an exchange opportunity.

We'll take a closer look at these in the HOW section. For now, start thinking about which city and where in that city you would like to live.

Rural retreat

If big skies and wide-open spaces put a smile on your dial, then rural living might be your happy place. Although a rural population is less concentrated than urban areas, there's still plenty of opportunity to find no-cost accommodation.

Rural rent-free living that I've personally experienced includes:

- farm sits
- property caretaking

- freedom camping, and
- volunteering for environmental or animal organisations or global groups like WWOOF.

Other rural opportunities for living rent-free involve seasonal jobs that include accommodation:
- agricultural work for harvest or planting seasons
- tourism and hospitality work during peak season.

Do these ideas pique your interest? You can find more detailed information about each type of Alt Accom in the HOW section of this book.

Exotic and unique locations

Now that you've already started to think outside the square on how to keep a roof over your head, why not go the extra step and consider unique locations.

Liquid lovers

Sorry guys, I'm not talking about wine, spirits or beer here. Although you could find seasonal work on vineyards that includes accommodation, this section is about water-based living. Whether you enjoy the open sea, large lakes or long rivers, a boat can be a home. Houseboats, yachts or cruising ships are the most common option. People who choose this lifestyle are often called live-aboards.

Landlubbers

Does the thought of literally living on water make you feel seasick? Maybe you enjoy being near water but prefer to keep your feet firmly on the ground. Island life might be a better option for you.

Caretaking on an island is a valid and viable choice. Tourism resorts, research stations and private property owners often seek the services of a caretaker. Not a fan of heat and sand? While we usually associate an island with swaying palm trees, sandy beaches and warm water, island lifestyle can also be found in cooler climates.

Digging deeper

If you want to keep digging in your quest for exotic and unique locations to live rent-free, underground or cave homes are a hidden gem. Stone-age surroundings with contemporary comforts can be found in places like:

- **Coober Pedy**, Australia. Here you might find a house sit, property to caretake or work that includes accommodation in the hospitality, retail or mining sector. There's a few freedom camping areas around the town (if you have you own self-contained RV). There's also an underground camping park which has site fees for those with tents or room rates for those needing a bed. An exchange opportunity may be available, where you provide housekeeping or other duties onsite in return for your 'rent'.
- **Cappadocia** region in Turkey. While researching this book, a house sit in a cave home owned by British expats was advertised on the HouseCarers website. Further research revealed there is a large tourism industry there and work in the hospitality sector could possibly include accommodation.

- **Saumur** in the Loire Valley, France. Rent-free living could be possible here by house sitting, property caretaking or seasonal work* related to harvesting truffles, snails, mushrooms and vineyards.

* *Research visas you may require for working in these countries.*

Woop-woop: remote locations

I was born and bred in the city. Easy access to arts and cultural experiences like galleries, libraries and theatre, helped shape my love of the arts. Hundreds of cafes, bars and restaurants to choose from on a daily basis, helped develop my foodie tastes. My city-based friends and family are always surprised when I wax eloquently about how much I love remote places. They know me as the café chick, the gallery hopper and the first one to try a new restaurant in town.

At the opposite end of the scale, volunteering work, personal projects and travelling in my RV have taken me to many places in remote wilderness areas or the outback.

A tropical jungle treehouse

The most remote Alt Accom I've lived in would have to be the stilt house on an island off Papua New Guinea (PNG). In my early twenties I spent two years there as a cross-cultural worker. Accommodation was provided onsite as the settlement was very remote. Rugen Harbour on New Britian Island was a 2-hour drive from the town of Rabaul.

The 'road' to town was a logging track accessible by 4WD only and required two river crossings. Infrastructure in such a remote place did not include bridges, so the river crossings were literally made by driving through the water. Depending on the season, the water could come up higher than the seats in the 4WD. This required taking a change of clothes, stored up high in the vehicle, so when we got to town, we could take our wet clothes off and have dry ones to wear while doing our shopping errands.

When it comes to remote living, that was about as remote as it gets. A shopping trip to town was a big occasion. An 8-hour adventure that not only entailed driving through crocodile-infested rivers, but slowly navigating rough dirt tracks through the mountains. Raskol gangs often dropped trees across the 'road' and held travellers at gunpoint while robbing and raping vehicle passengers.

That kind of remote living is not for the fainthearted, but I was 'young and dumb' back then and thought everything was a grand adventure. Many times, however, on those trips to and from Rabaul, with jungle pressing in close on both sides, the adventure wore thin. Little sparks of terror went through me every time I heard a tree fall somewhere up ahead. Thankfully our vehicle was never targeted by the Raskol gangs, but the threat of it loomed close the entire time. While I lived rent-free for two years in PNG, the cost to my nervous system was paid off slowly over several years.

The house I lived in rent-free, was on stilts in a clearing where the jungle met cocoa plantation trees. There were views down the hill through palm trees to the ocean. To the outsider's eye, I lived in a tropical paradise. The reality was slightly harsher. A generator provided power for 6 hours each day and the fridge ran on kerosene to keep a few things 'cold' in the humid tropical weather. Air conditioning was non-existent. The only way to cool off was under ceiling fans, or a quick dip in the ocean.

However, it wasn't all hardship. One benefit of living in the tropics was how easy it was to grow food. I had bananas, papaya, starfruit and pineapple growing around the house. Fruit salad was a staple diet. Snorkelling and scuba diving was spectacular with tropical fish and coral of many colours dancing through sunlit warm water.

My two years of living rent-free in PNG helped shape the person I am today. It laid the foundation for my love of travel, exploring other cultures and ways of living that are different to mainstream western society.

Lighthouse keeper or caretaker

Living rent-free at a lighthouse is still on my list, not yet ticked off, but I've started researching the options. Technological advances have seen most active lighthouses around the world become automatically operated. Ships also have such advanced navigation systems now, many lighthouses no longer operate as a safety warning like they used to. There are still some stations where a lighthouse is manned or has a caretaker.

Some caretaker roles fall into the category of accommodation provided with paid work. Some are volunteer positions where rent-free living in a remote location attracts nature lovers, writers, musicians and other creatives.

Many cottages once used by lighthouse keepers are now rented out as B&B accommodation and caretakers are onsite to manage that, rather than the lighthouse itself.

At the time of writing this (2023-24), I found the following locations you can still apply to live at a lighthouse:

Australia

In Australia, Parks Victoria employs up to 20 people as lighthouse keeper/caretakers at five lighthouses. The already remote state of Tasmania has the most southerly lighthouse in Australia on Maatsuyker Island. The lighthouse function there was fully automated in 1996, but volunteer caretakers live rent-free there for up to six months. The Tasmania Parks and Wildlife Service has standard and seasonal volunteer caretaker programs which includes Maatsuyker and six other locations.

Canada

There are 51 lighthouses in Canada that still require onsite staff. Hiring is done through Fisheries and Oceans Canada on behalf of the Canadian Coast Guard. Two jobs advertised at the time of writing had application closing dates of December 2023 and March 2024. The roles were paid and included rent-free accommodation.

USA

Five Finger Lighthouse in Alaska has helped ships navigate the state's legendary Inside Passage since 1902. Located on the southern island of the Five Finger group of islands, it still operates today as an active navigational aid. Volunteer lighthouse keepers live onsite for six months, April to September each year.

The Outback and beyond

If you'd rather be surrounded by a sea of sand or desert terrain, Outback Australia is known worldwide as being remote with minimal population. Despite that, there are numerous opportunities to live rent-free in the outback. Due to the remote locations, workers at roadhouses, sheep and cattle stations, or mining settlements are usually provided with free accommodation.

Property caretaking can provide a roof overhead at no cost, or a place to park up your RV for free. Landholders in remote areas often want a security presence on their land. Farmers look for caretakers to check on fences or feed livestock so they can travel for business, leisure or medical reasons.

5. This off-grid RV allowed a partner and I to avoid crowded expensive caravan parks and camp in luxury at remote places surrounded by natural beauty in outback Australia.

On a 6-month trip through the Red Centre of Australia, from Adelaide in the south to Darwin in the north, most nights were spent freedom camping. Having a self-contained RV meant the local environment was left in perfect condition. The only trace left was footprints (or tyre tracks). Sure, there is a cost to owning an RV and fuelling it up, but when you can park up for free in some of the world's most scenic yet remote areas, it can be cheaper than paying rent. Plus, the experience is much more interesting.

6

What about WORK?

How does work fit into the picture when choosing Alt Accom options? A common question people ask about living rent-free relates to working. One thing I learned was this; Slashing your expenses by cutting the cost of keeping a roof overhead, dramatically reduces how much you *need* to earn.

If you're already debt free, you can live very well on a lot less. So, if you don't need to earn as much, what would you do in that situation?

- Continue doing the same work, but only part-time.
- Continue as is and save a lot more money for the future.
- Start your own small business you can run from anywhere.
- Have a part-time job and a side-hustle.
- Change your job to something less stressful or more flexible.

Imagine if how many hours you work became a choice. When living rent-free, you don't **need** to work full-time hours if you don't want to. You can become semi-retired at any age. If you choose. Again, there's that word – choices.

Work remotely

Pre-pandemic, when remote work options were limited, I managed to find some organisations ahead of the curve who were already hiring talent regardless of where they lived. As a writer, designer and content creator, I could work from anywhere with internet coverage.

One good thing that's come out of the pandemic is the increase in employers willing to hire remote workers. The option to work remotely means you are no longer tied to living within commuting distance to a job. If you need to continue earning income while choosing to live rent- or mortgage-free, think about this. Can your existing job be done remotely? If not, what types of work can be done remotely, and can you pivot to one of those?

Portable work

Perhaps your skillset is portable. If you can pack your tools of the trade into your vehicle, then your options are huge. Services or trades that could be portable include:

- Hairdresser
- Massage therapist
- Electrician
- Mechanic.

Locums

Medical professionals can register with agencies for work opportunities away from their usual home or work location. Clinics need locum practitioners when the regular ones take vacation or sick leave. Options for work in these fields include:

- Nursing
- Doctor
- Dentist
- Chiropractor
- Physiotherapist.

In some places, accommodation may even be supplied as part of the package.

Seasonal work

When you start thinking outside the box on how to keep a roof over your head, it's worth doing the same about work. The status quo teaches us standard work routines like; 9-5 M-F, ongoing shift work or variations of that. But what if you prefer to work longer hours for a shorter time and take the rest of the year off?

One way to do that is with seasonal work. A variety of industries hire temporary casual staff to carry out work during their busy time of year. The type of work you might do seasonally includes:

Tourism and hospitality

Tourist destinations have peak and off-peak seasons. During the peak seasons, many businesses hire extra staff to cater for their busy time. When the peak season is depends on location. A ski resort's busy time is in winter, a beach resort's busy time is summer. Seasonal work in tourism and hospitality might include:

- Restaurant staff for front of house, kitchen and supplies.
- Accommodation staff for reception, cleaning, pool and garden maintenance.

- Instructor staff for snow skiing, surfing, golf, horse-riding.
- Transport staff for bus transfers, airport pickups or coach tours.

These jobs often include accommodation, which is one of the rent-free options already mentioned.

Temp Agencies

Temporary agencies help businesses find qualified employees for seasonal work. An accountant might hire extra staff for the busy tax return season. A not-for-profit might hire extra staff in the lead up to and during their annual fundraising campaign. Government agencies might hire extra staff to get a project completed on time.

Retail

Retail stores and distribution warehouses hire extra staff during peak shopping periods. Traditionally, in many countries, Christmas is the busiest shopping season in the year. Other busy shopping times are:
- Black Friday – USA, UK, Europe, South America, Australia
- Boxing Day – Australia, UK
- Singles Day – China, Europe
- Chinese New Year - China
- Diwali – India
- El Buen Fin – Mexico
- Valentines Day
- St Patricks Day
- Easter
- Mother's Day
- Father's Day

- Halloween
- Guy Fawkes Night - UK

Seasonal jobs in retail include cashier, shelf stocker, gift wrapper, warehouse staff – picking, packing, dispatch, store manager and retail assistant.

Delivery services

Peak times around holidays often mean an increased demand for delivery services. From retail goods to pizza, ordering online has become the norm. When the goods are ready for dispatch, someone has to deliver them to the customer. From truck to van or scooter, there's multiple opportunities to pick up delivery work.

Agriculture

Seasonal work is standard on farms. Work opportunities arise when crops need to be planted or harvested. Farms that raise livestock employ seasonal workers for things like shearing, mustering, drenching or droving. Large agricultural entities usually hire seasonal workers through agencies, smaller ones hire by word-of-mouth and the pub grapevine.

Wherever your adventures in alternative accommodation might take you, there's usually opportunities to earn an income along the way. Maintain the mindset of creative, out-of-the-box thinking, and you'll find there's a lot more to working life than the 9-5 or shift grind.

III

Part Three

7

HOW to live rent-free with the Alt Accom lifestyle

There are many ways to live rent-free. I spent eight years exploring them and have already shared some stories with you.

What you'll find in this section of the book, is hard-earned wisdom gained from my lived experience, along with pros and cons of each personally tested Alt Accom option. I've also included a couple of options I haven't personally tried (yet).

If one of them doesn't flip your switch, there will probably be another one that does. Somewhere in all this, you might find your own solution to the cost of keeping a roof overhead.

* * *

House sitting

My rent-free lifestyle started with two dogs. Lola and Nos. Their humans were friends of mine going on holiday. "Hey Kel, would you stay at our place and look after the dogs while we're away?"

Since my rental lease was about to end, it was great timing. I thought it would give me a couple of extra weeks to sort out my accommodation situation. In reality, it was the beginning of my adventures in Alt Accom.

My existing life in Melbourne didn't suffer as I could still commute to the office, shop at my local grocery store and catch up with my friends in the area. When I mentioned to friends I was house sitting, I suddenly had the next two months booked up with other sits.

House sitting for friends and family gave me experience, photo proof and references from happy home and pet owners. The next step was to become a registered sitter. I set up profiles on two house sitting websites and have now done sits in every state of Australia and some internationally. That fit perfectly with my dream to travel. But if you don't want to travel, it's easy to limit your sits to one location.

Whenever I picked up contract work, I would secure a sit in the city or town where that work was. When you save most of your income because you're not spending it on keeping a roof overhead, it's amazing how quickly you can build up a nice bank balance.

What exactly does a house sitter do?

A house sitter lives onsite in a home while the normal occupants are away. They generally provide:

- security
- pet care
- garden care

- mail collection
- basic maintenance.

House sitting doesn't mean homeless

Many sitters actually have their own home. They house sit as a way to travel and stay in different areas at no cost.

When the pandemic hit, international borders started to close. State borders came next, then travel stopped in its tracks. Because people couldn't travel, they didn't need sitters.

I bought a property with my partner in a rural area of South Australia and established a home base there. The smaller population of the state meant it was a safer refuge than the more populated eastern states. Apart from a few short lockdowns, we were relatively untouched by the worst of the pandemic. Travel was still allowed in that state, and a few house sits popped up. A work contract came up in the city, so I accepted a 3-month house sit. This allowed me to do the work contract and live rent-free within commuting distance of the office.

Was I homeless? No. I owned a property 3 hours out of the city.

A motorhome, caravan or campervan is also a type of of home that dovetails well with house sitting. At various stages of my journey, I've called each one of these my home. A common phrase in the nomad lifestyle is, "home is where we park it."

Fee or Free

There are two types of sitters. Those who charge money and those who do it as a win-win exchange service for rent-free living. Sometimes it may be a combination of the two. Money might change hands if you're also expected to carry out business related tasks like B&B cleaning or hours of farm work.

How you choose to sit is up to you and there are opportunities for both types. The most important thing is that both parties know and agree:

1. what the required work is before the sit commences
2. whether the sitter will charge a fee or not.

If you're considering charging a fee to house sit, you will need to cover all your legal business responsibilities like:

- choosing a business structure
- establish operating procedures
- organise insurances
- bookkeeping, taxes and more.

Personally, I'm an exchange sitter working in a win-win way. I don't charge a fee because the savings payoff -no rent or utility bills- is enough to sustain my simple lifestyle.

Negotiation is an important skillset as a house sitter. If you're asked to mind pets with complicated medical issues, anxious pets requiring constant company, multiple daily walks or very long walks, your freedom during the house sit is reduced. In situations like this, your ability to confidently negotiate extra items, will ensure a genuine win-win exchange. If cash is not offered or wanted, consider the following instead:

- owner provides use of vehicle for the duration of house sit
- owner organises someone else to mow the lawn or clean the pool
- sitter can use any fruit/veg/herbs from the garden to reduce grocery bills
- sitter can use meat from freezer (common on farms where they butcher their own)

- owner increases internet plan if not unlimited, so sitter can work remotely online
- *... think of something you might negotiate if the requirements of a sit went above normal pet feeding, gardening, or house care.*

Obviously, when deciding on fair exchange, consider the location of sit, equivalent rent in that area and so on. For example, in exchange for the opportunity to live like a local in a popular holiday destination, you might consider doing tasks you would not normally do at a house sit. Again, it is up to each house sitter and owner to come to a mutually agreed exchange.

Where to find house sits

Word of Mouth

When I started house sitting, just talking to people about what I was doing led to many opportunities. Happy clients told their friends about me, and my own network referred their friends and family to me.

Talking with neighbours or local people where I'm sitting, is another way to 'advertise'. Many have heard of house sitting, but until they meet a real live sitter, they don't connect how it might be helpful for them. I've had people ask for my card (which links them to my registered profile) and book me to do sits for them in the future.

Facebook

Personally, I have sourced some sits on local Facebook (FB) groups or pages. Experience has taught me that sits found here are usually short-term and have potential to be a nightmare. When a pet or homeowner chooses social media to source a sitter, it often reflects their lack of effort in communication, appreciation of a professional approach and understanding the etiquette of house sitting. Yes, that's a generalisation, but one my experience has informed me on.

My advice would be to always ensure a visit or video walk through first to "meet the animals." At the same time, you will learn more about the house, locality and owner. After that meet and greet, you are better equipped to decide if that sit suits you.

If you want to use FB to find house sits, there are many groups set up. Search in FB groups for "house sitting" "house sit." Many are targeted for local areas so include place names to find something specific. For example, "Australia" "Michigan" or "Niagara Falls". You'll find many such groups are full of sitters posting their availability. What you want are the ones where only owners can advertise for a sitter.

In Australia, one such group is "Aussie Housesitting Nomads." This group is hosted by a down-to-earth couple with years of sitting experience. They know the nomad lifestyle well and host the group to provide a space for fellow nomad sitters to connect with each other. Although the group's original aim was to be a support network for nomad sitters, owners are now allowed to join the group to advertise a sit they need help with.

House sit websites

Most house sits I've done were sourced from websites specifically aimed at helping home and pet owners find a registered sitter. Generally, it is free for a home or pet owner to advertise on these sites. Sitters pay annual fees to register on these websites, but it costs less than one night's accommodation in a hotel. Over an 8-year period, I've saved more than $100,000 on rent. That's an insanely good return on investment. What would **you** spend that money on?

Why register on a paid site

Professionalism

When you set up a profile on a registered sitters' website or app, you appear more professional. Even when you house sit for free as a win-win exchange, you can still be professional in the way you approach it. The most common feedback I have from owners is how much they appreciate my professional attitude.

Most sites allow reviews to be left by home and pet owners you've helped. This provides immediate social proof of being good at what you do.

When I first started house sitting, I did it for friends, family and workmates. While doing those sits, I took photos of the animals and most importantly, me with the animals. At the conclusion of those first few sits, I asked each of them for a written reference or their phone number for verbal references for future sits.

Quality clients

Owners who use a registered house sitting website or app (instead of Facebook etc) to find a are usually more intentional. What do I mean when I say that?

- They have put thought into what they need and who they want to fill that position.
- They have researched the options available to them.
- They see the value of s because sitters are presented in a professional way.
- They usually understand house sit etiquette and appreciate your service.

Avoid time wasters or potential nightmare house sits

After eight years of experience house sitting across Australia and the world, this is what I've learned. It's so easy for an owner to put a quick post on social media seeking a sitter. Little thought, small effort, vague info. Already, they are less invested than one who intentionally joins a house-sitting website to seek a sitter.

A house-sitting website is a specialised third party. It encourages accountability of owner and sitter. There is a record held by an invested third party of what the owner advertised and any communication between owner and sitter on the site. Accountability both ways is a win-win for owners and sitters.

Marketing made easy

House sitting websites or apps provide a platform for you to market your service. You can write a profile, share photos, reviews and other information that will help you stand out as the best choice.

It's easy to share a link to your profile page via text message, social media or in an email. You can even include a QR code on a business card. When someone scans it with their phone camera, your profile page will automatically open up.

Admin management tools

Another reason to join registered sitter sites is the inbuilt tools which help you manage the administrative side of your bookings. Each site varies, but management tools can include:

- **Messaging** – in the initial stages of enquiry, you can contact owners, or they can contact you via the inbuilt messaging system. Managing

enquiries is so much easier using the dedicated messaging section provided by a house sitting website or app.
- Notifications alert you when a message is received, and you can attend to them when you're free of distraction. This helps you present a professional manner to potential clients. There's nothing worse than getting a phone call when you're at the supermarket checkout, driving or focused on other work.
- Some inbuilt messaging platforms also have the option to save certain messages you might send. For example, you can set up a message that says, "Thanks for the invitation to consider your house sit. Unfortunately, I won't be in your area at that time." When you receive a request that doesn't work for you, a simple click or tap sends that message in response. Others have an auto decline button that sends a standard message the system generates.
- **Calendar** - record your bookings and availability on the inbuilt calendar.
- When you accept a sit advertised on some websites or apps, the dates are automatically added to your calendar on the site. Some also include automatic date alignment built into their calendar. For example, sits that clash with dates already booked on your calendar won't show up for you. This helps simplify the process for you and owners. It helps you avoid double-booking yourself and helps owners see who is available for the dates they need a sitter.
- **Locations** – being registered as a sitter on a website also makes it easier for you to find sits in specific locations. Search parameters can include, country, state, city/town or even include a map that shows people looking for a within the dates you select.
- **Reviews** – another reason to register with a house sitting website or app is the inbuilt review system. When you complete a sit booked on that site, you can easily receive references from happy owners whose home or pet you looked after. Excellent references or reviews

will give other owners confidence in booking you. Word-of-mouth advertising works best. People like to choose people who've proven to be good at what they do.

Set up your sitter profile

Write a bio that tells a little about why you're house sitting, any specialist experience you offer and why you are the best choice. Write it all from the perspective of what the client wants (yes, it's about you, but ultimately, it's about the client).

When setting up your profile, remember this, Marketing 101 – it's all about your customer or client. What do they want, what fears do they have, what pain points? How do you help, why are you the best choice?

I've spent years working in the marketing communications industry. Most businesses and individuals, when selling themselves, usually talk too much about just that, themselves. Yes, it's important to establish that you can provide what the client wants or needs, but when writing about yourself, tell the story in a way that addresses what a client is looking for.

Photos – Include photos of you with animals, working in gardens or on a farm. Share photos that show you engaging in work such as house cleaning/maintenance, gardening, farming or animal care.

A selection of happy snaps showing you in various holiday destinations is not what the owner wants to see. Home and pet owners want to see you doing things they need done. Give them visual proof that you're capable of doing the tasks required to keep their home and pets in good condition while they are away.

6. This photo of me walking dogs on a sit, provides pictorial proof of what I will do with prospective client's pets, if they choose me as their sitter.

Photos like this help build credibility. You will stand out from the 'tourist only' sitters who just want free accommodation at a popular holiday destination. Show owners that you take sitting responsibilities seriously. That's how you stand out from the crowd.

References and reviews – if you are new to house sitting and don't yet have a reference or review, you could include reviews from other platforms. If you have reviews from Airbnb, Couchsurfing, Wwoofing, HelpX or others, include copies of reviews from hosts there. Those reviews will show homeowners you are capable of treating other's property with respect and care. The other option is to mind friends' pets or gardens when they go away for a weekend or longer. Get a written review off them and include in your profile.

How to apply for a sit

Read the ad. Ensure location, duration, dates, animal care, garden care or other responsibilities match your skills and interests. View photos. If there are none, request some. You have provided photos on your profile. Expect equal sharing of information. House sitting is an exercise in building trust, on both sides. Some owners say they don't want photos of their home on the internet. That's fine, give them your email address.

Apply for the sit. In your first message or phone call let the homeowner know why you're the best choice for them. Are you great with cats? Have experience on farms? Do you have proof of your house sitting experience in the form of reviews provided by happy home or pet owners? Or specific photos of you carrying out tasks they need?

Meet & greet. This is where owners and sitters meet. It may be in person at the property or via a video call. Voice-only phone calls are not ideal. You want to see the property, the state of the home, garden, the pets or animals etc. If you can't visit in person, a video call is the next best option.

After a year of house sitting, I realised I was asking the same questions at every meet & greet. They would verbally tell me things, and I would try to write notes or remember details. To simplify the process, I created a House Sitter Checklist.* Instead of focusing on small details during the meet & greet, the focus can be on connecting with the owners, animals and getting a basic feel for the sit. I now tell owners that if they choose me to do their sit, I will send them a checklist for all the details. Owners love the checklist and say it helps them organise their information into a simple format.

* The House Sitter Checklist is available in the Resources section.

Agreement. If owners select you as their sitter, ask them to fill in your Checklist (before you accept the sit). Say, *"Once you've completed the checklist and returned it to me, I can then confirm the sit and enter it into the calendar."* This <u>one step</u> provides you with a:

- **written document** in which the owner details their needs, dates, location and more. Some people use contracts, personally I think that's too formal. A checklist is a friendlier way to gain all the details of what they require. If any issues come up during or after the sit, you have something in writing about the agreed exchange.
- **quick one-stop reference tool.** A reminder when you start the sit, of all the tasks they want covered, emergency contacts, and more. Having information in one place is invaluable and much more reliable than memory or accessing information scattered through text messages, emails or phone calls.
- **confirmation** that the owners are equally invested in the process, respect your worth as a sitter and take their responsibility to provide correct information seriously. If an owner baulks at completing the checklist, or doesn't send it back completed, take that as a red flag. If they often have sitters and already have their own document full of information, I tell them to note on the checklist, "see other document" and ask them to send a copy of their own document also.

Confirm in your calendar. On receipt of their completed checklist, you have the information needed to make your final commitment to the sit. Confirm the sit with owners and add sit to your calendars (house sitting websites should have this as part of your admin tools - it shows others looking for sitters that you're already booked for certain dates.)

Touch base one week prior to the sit and confirm the date and time of your arrival.

House sitting websites

There are many websites which help owners find sitters and vice versa. My recommendations come from 10 years of personally using these platforms.

After trying a few, I narrowed it down to the following two groups:

The **House Sitters Group** is an international group with five websites catering to different countries. Each website in this larger group works on the same layout design. So, if you choose to travel the world with house sitting, you don't have to learn a new interface for each country.

Australia www.aussiehousesitters.com.au
New Zealand www.kiwihousesitters.co.nz
Canada www.housesitterscanada.com
USA www.housesittersamerica.com
UK www.housesittersuk.co.uk

An advantage with this group of sites is that any reviews you receive can be linked to other sites within their group. For example, I have reviews from sits I did in Canada, that show on my Australian profile. Owners have often commented on those international reviews as a positive thing. They see it as giving more weight to my credentials as an experienced house sitter. See the **Reader Bonus** section for a discount joining fee for readers of this book.

Mindahome has two websites which cover some countries in the southern and northern hemisphere.

Australia www.mindahome.com.au
UK www.mindahome.co.uk

RV or vanlife

Mobile homes have been used as Alt Accom for decades. Canvas-covered wagons carried pioneers across countries like America, South Africa and Australia. Richly decorated vardos (commonly called Gypsy wagons) carried artists, showmen and other creatives around Europe.

In an everything-old-is-new-again switcheroo, #vanlife and #RVlife has gone mainstream. From simple campervans to offroad caravans and fully self-contained motorhomes, there's a house on wheels to suit most people. Once thought of as a short-term holiday or relocation option, the road trip has extended into a new way of living.

The pandemic injected a boost into the RV industry. Travel restrictions saw people choose local road trip adventures instead of flights to far-off places. Post pandemic, the skyrocketing costs of keeping a roof overhead, has seen RVs come into their own as an Alt Accom option.

Gone Wheelabout – tales from the road

My own journey into the RV lifestyle began 5 years before the pandemic. house sitting gave me a taste of rent-free living. One day I realised that owning a mobile home would neatly dovetail into the house sitting ventures. While I've had house sits of 3-6 months in duration, many are shorter. Realising a mobile home would keep a roof overhead in between house sits, I started small and moved my way through a few different styles. I have owned the following mobile homes or RV's:

- Campervan
- Motorhome
- Caravan

There's not much I don't know about living the RV lifestyle. Through personal trial and error, I learned what worked for me and what didn't. Here's some of what I've learned.

Living in a house on wheels is a lot cheaper than paying a mortgage or renting. House sitting allowed me to save rent money so I could buy a campervan. It was a simple affordable start. A vehicle small enough to easily drive around and park in a city. A bed, table, and cooking area included an oven, stovetop, and fridge. The cost of registration, insurance and maintenance on the campervan cost a lot less than rent. I had a membership with a chain of gyms opened 24/7 which provided me space to exercise and a hot shower.

You can grow as you go. I started with a campervan, upgraded to a motorhome, then bought a caravan with a partner. The extra money I saved while living on wheels, was able to slowly fund an improvement in my mobile accommodation. Each step came with better facilities on board. What you need as an 'essential' onboard will be different to what someone else needs. What you consider essential may also change depending on your stage of life, how many passengers you have or the location you are travelling in.

Going off grid is an investment in future comfort. Sure, setting up solar power comes with a cost. But that pays for itself quickly when you don't have to plug into mains power. When your home on wheels is self-contained, you carry your own water, power and toilet onboard. This helps you avoid paying high fees at caravan parks and keeps ongoing expenses lower.

A house on wheels doesn't have to move. Just because a mobile home has wheels, that doesn't mean you have to keep driving it around. If you don't want to travel, there are plenty of options for where to park up and stay put in one place.

It's doable on any budget. For a very short time, my mobile 'home' was a station wagon (estate car). Low entry level price, plenty of storage and space for a bed in the back. I know people who permanently live out of a tiny hatchback car while travelling. While I gave it a go as a gap-filling option, my experience in the station wagon taught me I needed a more practical setup that included room to stand up, cook and clean. So, while a micro camper car wasn't ideal for me, other people find it works for them. Like most things, it comes back to what your goal is and what you're prepared to do to achieve it.

Home away from home

Hmm, the concept of someone living in a vehicle raises another question. What does it mean to be homeless? At first glance people assume a rent-free lifestyle means being homeless. I'm here to prove that is not always the case.

Let me share a few stories that will put that idea to rest. My personal experience includes living rent-free while, at one stage having an apartment and another, a rural property.

Vanlife doesn't mean homeless

A small campervan was my introduction to the RV lifestyle in 2015. During the time I owned it, I had established a home base in a rented apartment while working a corporate city contract. Simple trips from A to B, and weekend getaways gave me an introduction to van life. I enjoyed it so much, I wondered if I could make a mobile home my permanent roof overhead.

How could I try this out without losing my existing home space?

The answer I came up with was to sublet my apartment for a short time. This covered home-base expenses while giving me freedom to do a test run of RV life. A young couple had been sponsored into the country by their employer, but needed a short-term home until they found their own. It was a win-win. They were happy, my fully furnished apartment was an instant home for them when they arrived with two suitcases. I was happy having all my bills covered. It freed up my cash to buy a self-contained motorhome and I set off on a longer RV trip.

While out on the road, I contacted them to see if they'd found a place of their own yet. No. I asked if they'd like to extend the sublet for 3 months. Yes.

After a few months living the nomad life, I checked back in with them. They loved the apartment, the location and were having trouble finding something just as good. I asked if they'd like to stay on. *Yes!*

So, while my home-base was being used to help others establish themselves in a new country, I had the freedom to complete a risk-free trial of living in a motorhome for a year. The savings I made on not having to pay rent, or store my furniture somewhere, allowed me to upgrade to a proper motorhome. Without losing my established home-base for me to come back to.

Roaming retirees

Inspired in part by my own adventures, one set of parents wanted to spend time exploring their own country. They own a great house with a pool on the lakefront. But after years of international travel, work and living, they tossed their keys to tenants and hit the road with a caravan. Now that's what I call a win-win. Happy tenants, happy homeowners.

So, there you have it. Not everyone who chooses Alt Accom options is homeless. Some of us do it by choice. We value the savings made and freedoms gained if we put tenants in our home.

Freedom camping

Depending on where you live or travel, freedom camping may also be called free camping, boondocking, off-grid camping or wild camping.

When choosing an RV for your rent-free lifestyle, an important consideration is being self-contained. This term is often used to describe an RV set up to "leave no trace" apart from footprints or tyre tracks. For most, this means having a kitchen and toilet on board. After eight years, my definition of self-contained also includes having enough power and water to live off-grid comfortably for more than a couple of nights.

Choosing the right RV for you

How do you know which RV will work best for you? This section will focus on the three main types of RV – Motorhomes, Caravans or Campervans. There are other options such as camper trailers, roof-top tents and tear-drop style caravans, but I have no lived experience with them.

When you start thinking about using an RV as your Alt Accom, there are so many things to consider. Here's a short comparative list to get you started:

Advantages	Disadvantages
Campervan	
Cheaper way to start off	Harder for long term living
Fits in standard parking space	Many you can't stand up in
Better fuel economy	Most are not self-contained (no bathroom)
Stealth camping possible	Limited storage space
Caravan	
Can leave camp with tow car only	More setup and pack up
Cheaper option if already have tow-car	Complex van and vehicle weight ratios
Storage space in car and caravan	Harder to park and manoeuvre
Motorhome	
Everything under one roof	Reduced fuel economy than campervan
Easy and quick to stop and set up	Once setup camp, stuck there
Security with access front cab to back	Expensive runaround in town
Self-contained with bathroom	Water in tanks increases travel weight
Rooftop deck may be possible	Height restrictions limit some routes

7. *Comparative chart for three types of RV (mobile home).*

Try before you buy

Before spending large amounts of money, it's a good idea to hire a van of choice for a weekend or week away. There's nothing like living in one to help you realise what you do and don't want. Look for commercial hire companies, or private people renting their own vans out through sites like Camplify in Australia, New Zealand, UK and Spain.

If the cost of commercial retail hire is too prohibitive, consider doing a relocation. Recreational van hire companies offer the opportunity to experience vanlife for as little as $1 a day, plus fuel expenses. When a full paying customer rents a vehicle one way, or the rental company needs to move stock to different areas, they use this method as a win-win. You get to drive a van from one destination to another at a very low cost, and they get their vehicles relocated at low cost. These are only one-way trips, so you need alternative options to return home.

Some of the sites which facilitate van relocations include:
www.transfercar.com.au

This group offers transfers in Australia, New Zealand, America, South Africa and Brazil for hire companies such as Hertz, SIXT and Enterprise. You'll find the links to each country's site at the bottom of the website's home page.

www.imoova.com

This site coordinates van transfers for more than 150 hire companies like Apollo, Avis, Britz, Indie Campers, Jucy Rentals, Wicked Campers and Travellers Autobahn. One-way van transfers can be organised in Europe, Canada, USA, NZ, and Australia. You'll find the links to each country's site at the bottom of the website's home page.

* * *

Property caretaking

Another way to cut the cost of keeping a roof overhead is to become a property caretaker. Accommodation might be provided in the form of a house, cabin, unit or a site to park your RV and connect to power/water.

What is caretaking?

There are two main types of property caretaking: land-based and commercial-based. **Land-based property caretaking** generally involves larger farm or personal land holdings and is less focused on domestic pets than house sitting. There may be some livestock related tasks like keeping water troughs clean and full, moving stock to different paddocks for fresh grass supply or repairing any damage to fencing. Very often though, property caretaking is more about the land. Tasks could include:

- Clearing fallen trees or branches and stacking it for future firewood.
- Slashing or mowing around buildings and alongside tracks.
- Running water pumps or farm machinery.
- Maintaining a residence to keep it clean, aired out and in good working order while owners are away.
- Sometimes just providing a security presence to discourage theft or wilful damage.

Commercial property caretaking usually involves properties that deliver hospitality services, rental accommodation and more. This type of caretaking can be found in urban and regional areas. Tasks that might be required of a commercial property caretaker include:

- Maintenance duties like building repairs, pool servicing, snow shovelling or garbage.
- Gardening duties like mowing lawns and weeding.
- Housekeeping duties like cleaning rooms between guests.
- Hospitality duties like checking guests in and out.

The basic skillset required to get started as a property caretaker is someone who is independent, resourceful and practical. The type of property will determine any specific skillsets, training or qualifications required.

Where to find caretaker opportunities

The list of properties that might need a caretaker is enormous. To help you explore this idea, here's some potential places:
- farms and ranches
- private estates
- private islands
- recreational camps
- hunting and fishing lodges
- holiday resorts and homes
- tenanted apartment blocks
- retirement villages
- historic properties, and
- educational campuses.

While these might not be your standard caretaker gig, you might be lucky enough to find something exotic or totally outlandish like a Tropical island caretaker or A monarch and pub owner on an island.

How to find a gig

Property owners advertise for caretakers in many ways, word-of-mouth, in print, or online.

Word-of-mouth

If you're on the ground in an area you'd like to live, ask at the local pub/hotel, feed and grain store or farm machinery sales or repair yard.

Printed ads

Less common these days, printed ads for caretakers can still be found. Community noticeboards allow people to post cards or posters with their ad. Again, like word-of-mouth, it's easier to find printed ads for caretaker opportunities when in the local area.

Online

The *Caretaker Gazette* started off as a printed newsletter in 1983 and has now moved online as well. Based in the USA, it has more caretaking opportunities in USA, Canada and Alaska, however ads sometimes include places like Australia, Hawaii, Europe and the UK.

Other websites that advertise caretaker opportunities include:

- house sitting sites
- Employment sites
- And online community noticeboards.

* * *

Exchange Volunteering

Work exchange is what happens when someone (host) needs help with tasks and someone else volunteers to help. In exchange for their labour, volunteers (helpers) are provided with accommodation and meals by the host.

8. In exchange for work on a blueberry farm in WA, I stayed in this cottage, received some meals and as many berries as I could eat.

Family farms or households are the most common places offering exchange opportunities. The platform I've personally had experience with is the original help exchange network WWOOF https://wwoofinternational.org/ and https://wwoof.com.au/ in Australia.

I spent time on an organic blueberry farm in Western Australia, helping a mum and dad with two kids. While there I helped them establish a new section of berry plants, installed and monitored irrigation systems, planted blueberry bushes and other farm related tasks.

Another WOOOF experience I had was staying in a spare room of a couple's mud-brick home and working in their permaculture garden, weeding, harvesting produce and cooking chutneys to stock the pantry.

While my initial reason for joining WWOOF was to seek Alt Accom options, in the process of working closely with those families, I learned new land and animal skills. I also formed ongoing friendships that have enriched my life.

Where to find exchange opportunities

Here are some places online you can find exchange gigs where you will receive accommodation and sometimes meals for your helping hands.
HelpX https://www.helpx.net/
Workaway https://www.workaway.info/
Worldpackers https://www.worldpackers.com/
HippoHelp https://hippohelp.com/
Volunteers Base https://www.volunteersbase.com/

* * *

Job that includes accommodation

I was only 19 when I had my first rent-free living experience. As a live-in nanny, I received accommodation and meals on top of my pay. Yeah, the pay wasn't great, but with no living expenses, I saved money towards a diploma course I started the following year.

Jobs that might provide accommodation include:
- personal carer
- private housekeeper
- hospitality / tourism
- nanny / au-pair
- property caretaker
- lighthouse caretaker
- greens keeper
- roadhouse staff
- seasonal farm work like harvesting or shearing.

Most large employment websites have great search facilities. Type in the words "live in", or "accommodation provided" and a list of suitable job ads will come up.

* * *

All aboard - floating homes

This type of Alt Accom is still on my personal 'to do" list. I grew up around boats, and have spent hours on catamarans, speed boats, yachts and motor boats. While I've slept overnight in yacht cabins and houseboats, I've not yet made a boat my home. Now that I've experienced off-grid living in RV's, a floating home might be my next adventure. If the idea appeals to you, here's some ways to get on board.

BYO boat

Marine based Alt Accom options include being a live-aboard on a houseboat, yacht or cruiser. Obviously, there's an initial outlay and ongoing maintenance costs. Just like when you own a land-based mobile home or RV. However, the costs are usually much less than buying and maintaining your own house, unit or property. There are places you can freely moor and live on a boat. New technologies that produce power and drinking water, now make living off grid on the water very comfortable. Rules and regulations of mooring, waste management and length of stay are different everywhere.

Cruise ship and yacht charter crew

Yacht charters and cruise ships require crew to serve their clients while onboard. A berth is usually supplied as part of the package and you can find work as a deckhand, galley cook, housekeeper, entertainer or beautician.

Boat relocation crew

Boat owners sometimes hire ongoing crew to relocate their boat to different ports. They or their guests fly and board the boat in the new location, rather than taking the offshore trip. Sometimes this is a paid opportunity, other times it's a free travel opportunity to increase your offshore navigation skills and sea log hours.

* * *

Artist in residence - for creatives

Artist residencies are offered by hosting organisations or communities who provide space and resources to support individual artistic practice. They offer artists – musicians, visual artists, writers – the opportunity to work in a new environment, free from the constraints of daily life, to develop their work and explore new ideas creatively.

Public and private organisations offer residency for artists and can include:
- National parks
- Museums
- Libraries
- Arts organisations
- Historic trust properties
- Private homes and studio spaces.

You can also search the following websites for global Artist-in-residence opportunities:

https://resartis.org/

This Worldwide Network of Arts Residencies is the leading international Member-network of arts residencies. On this website you will find some 650 member organisations from 80 countries offering artist residencies.

https://www.artconnect.com/opportunities/residencies?sortBy=-deadline&types=ART_RESIDENCY

Along with global opportunities for artists, Art Connect also presents useful guides on how to prepare a submission to receive a residency.

Artist residencies are sometimes advertised in shops who sell products to that type of artist. For example, art stores, bookstores or craft stores.

* * *

After learning about seven types of Alt Accom that could help you live a rent-free lifestyle, you might be wondering which one would work best for you. The next chapter holds a questionnaire to point you in the right direction.

8

QUIZ: Find your best fit

Wondering which type of Alt Accom would work best for you.? Here's some questions to think about. Your answers will point you in the right direction. They may even highlight a unique combination that will perfectly suit you and your needs.

How adventurous are you?
1. Very adventurous! Exchange volunteering could be your thing. The huge variety of work and accommodation combinations across the world, offers limitless adventures.
2. Somewhat adventurous. RV, vanlife or floating homes offer you the ability to roam, with most comforts of home onboard.
3. Not adventurous at all. House sitting would be a good choice for you. All the comforts and convenience of a home, without the expense.

What's your budget?
1. I have a flexible budget. A combination of RV life and house sitting or property caretaking allows for reducing fuel costs or site fees.

This is handy for those times you need to slow down your spending.
2. I'm on a tight budget. If travel is important to you, a combination of vanlife and exchange volunteering can be one of the most affordable ways to keep a roof overhead. Alternatively, if travel is not important, a job that provides accommodation could be the best option for you.
3. Money is not a concern. Your own luxury RV or yacht gives you the ability to travel where you want.

How long do you plan to stay in the accommodation?
1. Short-term (a few weeks to a few months). Artist-in-residence programs or exchange volunteering could suit you.
2. Medium-term (several months to a year). Vanlife is generally suitable for shorter time periods. Living in a small vehicle can work well in combination with house sitting. If you need to earn money, a job with accommodation might suit you best.
3. Long-term (more than a year). RV life, a house boat, property caretaking or house sitting are good longer-term alternative accommodation options.

What's your packing style?
1. Have backpack or suitcase and will travel. House sitting, exchange volunteering or jobs that include accommodation are great options for the intrepid traveller.
2. Want to pack everything, including the kitchen sink. A self-contained RV, houseboat or yacht provides the daily essentials along with plenty of space to store your stuff.
3. Flexible to suit the situation. A combination of your own mobile home, with a suitcase or backpack ready to go, gives you the best

of both worlds. A home-base and the option to travel more lightly when you want for leisure or work opportunities.

Do you enjoy taking care of a property or animals?

1. Yes, I love it! House sitting would be a great fit for you. Caring for pets in their own home provides plenty of opportunity for time with furry friends. Plus, you usually get to garden too.
2. I'm open to it. Property caretaking on farms often includes the less hands-on care of farm animals. Land management or property management skills are also required.
3. Not really. Live-aboard opportunities on boats do not involve animal care or mowing lawns.

What's your preferred level of independence?

1. Complete independence. An RV or boat set up for off-grid living can be a complete tiny home, either travelling or pulled up in one spot.
2. Some interaction with others. House sitting and property caretaking involves liaising with property owners and sometimes other staff. However, you usually have privacy in the accommodation. Staying in caravan parks involves close neighbours and shared bathroom or kitchen facilities if your RV or van is not set up with those facilities.
3. I prefer communal living. Exchange volunteering often involves living within a family home, or with others in a shared space.

Remember this:
There is no one right way to keep a roof over your head. That's the whole premise of this book!

I've spent the best part of a decade exploring multiple options. What works for you will vary, depending on current life circumstances and personal preferences.

The next and final section of this book offers more guiding questions and step-by-step processes to help you get started on your own alternative accommodation journey. This is where the rubber meets the road, and you start to put your own action plan in place.

IV

Part Four

9

RESOURCES - From dreaming to doing

Right about now, you might be looking for a sign. If you've read the whole book (and not just skipped to the end for the summary) that's your sign! Something in this book has got you thinking. Maybe even dreaming again. You can see a solution to your problem.

Is it possible - could you actually escape the time and money trap?

Absolutely. These viable alternatives to the mainstream way of keeping a roof overhead, can help you live free of rent or a mortgage and achieve goals and dreams that previously felt impossible.

Dreams can come true, but you need to put an action plan in place.

Are you ready to say, "Stuff the status quo!"?

Righto, let's do this!

Action sheets

The following pages provide you with you hands-on practical ways to **decide, determine** and **do** the Alt Accom lifestyle. Along with the exercises provided in earlier chapters, these activities will help you make choices that best align with your circumstances and personal goals. You know what your dreams are. Here are the tools to help you do what's required to get them:

- First Steps
- **Decide** what your starter style is
- **Determine** which Alt Accom suits you
- **Do** these three things – secure, sell, store
- Mail sorted
- RV quiz
- Checklist
- **Reader bonus** – discount code for websites

First steps

There are three stepping stones to get you started.

Decide what your starter style is.

- **Dip your toes** - Do you want to do it short term as a taster (a holiday or between rental lease) to see if it might work longer term later?
- **Deep dive** – Do circumstances, or your courage, demand a fast immersion into alternative accommodation?

Determine which Alt Accom suits your situation.

If you need to stay in one area for work, family or other commitments:

- House sitting – opportunities are everywhere and geographically searchable through dedicated websites.

If mobility and the freedom to travel are very important, consider:
- RV or vanlife - Ideal if you want to move frequently and explore different locations.
- Exchange volunteering - Offers the opportunity to travel and stay in various places for short periods.

If you want accommodation with work or responsibilities:
- Property caretaking - Suitable for those willing to take on caretaking responsibilities in exchange for accommodation.
- Job that Includes Accommodation - Will provide a place to stay.

If you need or prefer spacious and well-equipped living areas:
- House sitting - Provides the comfort of a full home in exchange for maintenance duties, garden or pet care.
- RVs in the luxury motorhome style could fit the bill here.

If being part of a community or socialising is very important:
- Artist-in-residence - Often includes community engagement and opportunities to showcase and share your work and process.
- Exchange volunteering - Allows for social interaction with hosts and other volunteers.

If you enjoy being surrounded by nature or water:
- Floating homes - Offers a unique living experience on the water.
- RV or vanlife - Allows for stays in natural settings.
- Property caretaking on an island or farm could be ideal.

If on a tight budget for accommodation:
- Exchange volunteering - Accommodation is often provided at low or no cost, in exchange for labour or work.
- Property caretaking - Can also offer free or low-cost living arrangements.

If planning a short-term stay:
- House sitting - Often short-term, ranging from days to a few months.
- Exchange volunteering - In exchange for work, short term accommodation is usually provided and sometimes includes meals.

If you have specific skills or experience beneficial for certain types of accommodation:
- Property caretaking - Maintenance, gardening or farm skills.
- Artist-in-residence - Artistic skills are essential.

If personal goals include exploring new lifestyles and cultures:
- Exchange volunteering - Allows for cultural exchange and learning new ways of living.
- International house sitting – lets you live like a local in exchange for home, garden or pet care.

Determine if a combination of Alt Accom might suit you. For example, if you value mobility, community, and have a tight budget, vanlife combined with exchange volunteering could be the perfect combination. If you enjoy large living spaces, some mobility and cultural exchange, international house sitting or property caretaking opportunities might work best for you.

Do these three things.

1. Secure an opportunity to live in Alt Accom. Book a house sit / Buy or hire RV or van / Apply for work that provides accommodation as part of the package.
2. Sell or lease your existing home.
3. Store, sell and pack for your new accommodation lifestyle.

10

Letting stuff go – how to declutter and simplify

One of the main questions people have when considering Alt Accom is; "What do I do with all my stuff?"

Once you've made the decision to live free of rent or mortgage, short or long term, the next step is a very practical and essential one. This is why I call it a *lifestyle.* It's a choice that reaches into many parts of your life.

Decluttering, simplifying, and reducing the amount of stuff you need to live comfortably, is a mental and physical process. It helps if you approach it in a methodical way.

Sort your things

The easiest way I've found to sort and declutter is a simple three-pile system. Also have a garbage bin or box in the room. The bin is not a pile. It's a non-retrievable container for things past their use-by-date, broken, or no longer needed. Your definition of items to be thrown out will vary from mine. The key is to be decisive.

Tackling one room at a time, create three piles:
- Pile 1: Keep to store
- Pile 2: Pack to take with you
- Pile 3: Sell or donate

Storage

If you plan to put things in storage, consider the costs versus benefits. When I first started the Alt Accom adventure, I kept a lot of things in storage with the following methods:

Portable storage. Taxi Box delivered a portable storage box to my property, I packed things into the box (like a shipping container), they picked it up and took it to their storage facility. When I wanted to re-establish a home base, they delivered the box to my new address, where I unpacked it. This option avoided double handling, allowed plenty of space for a house lot of furniture and provided easy delivery on demand to any city in the country. https://www.taxibox.com.au/

Self-storage units were a lot more work, involving double handling at both ends. Packing stuff into a trailer or vehicle, driving it to the storage location, and unpacking it all into the storage unit. The process was reversed when ending the storage time.

Onsite. When I sublet my city apartment, I stored some things in the garage and the rest was part of the turnkey lease, fully furnished for the tenant.

Storage fees vary depending on size and location. After a few years, I realised it was a waste of money to store things that could easily be replaced in future. I also learned items can be damaged in long term storage through heat, humidity, insects, animals and more.

Downsizing was my preferred option and I only kept what I could take with me. I sold and donated/gifted everything I'd been paying to store. Not only did I save money on storage fees, I made money selling things off. A double win.

Packing

The type of Alt Accom you choose will determine what items you need to keep and pack for the journey. From "everything including the kitchen sink," to "bare basics in a backpack," knowing how much to pack is a key part of enjoying your adventures.

If you have an RV, a mini home of sorts, you will need utensils, tools, linen and other items just like at home. Not as many of course, but a condensed version.

On the other end of the scale, if you're going to house sit, all you really need is a suitcase or backpack with your own personal basics.

Sell, gift, donate

The items you put in your sell or donate pile will still be in good condition. Facebook marketplace or other online sales lists make it easy to sell stuff. Other ways to sell include yard sales, auctions, markets and on consignment.

Consider gifting things which have sentimental or special value to a family member or friend. When emotionally attached to an item, giving it to someone close is one way of keeping it within your 'circle.'

When I moved from one side of Australia to the other, I donated many things to a local project helping homeless people. Along the way I've donated stuff to opshops (thrift stores) to help a charity raise funds and allow people on a tight budget to afford some nice things.

Mail sorted

Managing your mail while living in Alt Accom ensures you keep track of personal letters, bills and other hard copy written communication. The easiest way to handle mail is;

- **Move current incoming post to email not snail mail.** Contact all your service providers, membership organisations and others who post you mail. Change your preferred method to email.
- **PO Box if staying in one area.** Rent a box at the local post office. This is the most secure way to receive hard copy mail.
- **For small budgets and small post offices.** Introduce yourself to staff and let them know you will be receiving some post restante (c/- post office) mail.
- **Residential address** hack. If you must provide a residential address for driver's licence or other formal mail, ask a family/friend to borrow their address as a temporary measure.

11

RV Quiz

TAKE THIS QUIZ to get an RV recommendation. Circle the points for each correct response, then add your points to get a total score.

Mobility and size:
I prefer a large fully self-contained drivable vehicle. (1 point)
I'm comfortable with towing a separate vehicle. (2 points)
I prefer a compact, drivable vehicle. (3 points)

Space and accommodation:
I need a separate living area from the driver's cab, with walkthrough access and good storage options. (1 point)
I'm comfortable with a living area in a different vehicle, with separate sections. (2 points)
I can make do with a smaller, more integrated living space. (3 points)

Amenities and comfort:
I require full amenities, including a kitchen, bathroom, and sleeping quarters. (1 point)
I need amenities like kitchenette and bathroom but can compromise on space. (2 points)

I'm okay with minimal amenities and can handle simple living conditions. (3 points)

Budget and expenses:

I have a generous budget for purchasing and maintaining an RV. (1 point)

I have a moderate budget and am willing to invest in a quality RV. (2 points)

I have a tight budget and need an affordable option for full-time living. (3 points)

Climate considerations:

I need an RV that is well-insulated and suitable for all seasons. (1 point)

Climate control is important, but I can manage with moderate insulation. (2 points)

I can adapt to different climates and don't require extensive climate control. (3 points)

Community and connectivity:

I prefer staying in RV parks with social opportunities and WIFI. (1 point)

I'm comfortable with RV parks and remote locations but need reliable internet. (2 points)

I prefer remote locations and can manage with limited connectivity. (3 points)

Long-term durability:

I need an RV built to withstand full-time living for several years. (1 point)

Durability is important, but I'm open to less expensive options. (2 points)

I'm considering full-time RV living as a temporary arrangement. (3 points)

Resale value and future plans:

Resale value is important as I may consider selling the RV in the future. (1 point)

I'm not overly concerned about resale value, but I may sell the RV eventually. (2 points)

I'm more focused on immediate needs and not worried about resale. (3 points)

Scoring:

Generally speaking, this is how the scores work:

The lower the score, the more suitable a motorhome might be for your needs.

If the score is somewhere in the middle, a caravan may be your best option.

The higher the score, you might find a campervan could be your most appropriate choice.

12

House Sitter Checklist

Here is a copy of the **House Sitter Checklist** I created. After you've had a meet and greet about a house sit and wish to continue, ask the home/pet owners to complete the checklist. This will provide you with written confirmation of location, dates and expected duties.

From nearly a decade of doing this, the stats show that if they don't provide the details requested, you (the sitter) will face challenges on the assignment. Tell them you can only confirm the sit and add dates to your booking calendar on receipt of the completed checklist.

* * *

House sitter checklist

Dear homeowners,

This checklist will make it easier for you to prepare information before you go away. It will also help me understand your expectations and ensure we're all on the same page.

Please answer each question that is applicable and email it back to me on _____

If you often have sitters and use your own house manual or other document, simply note next to any items on this checklist, "refer to house manual" etc and attach your document along with this completed checklist.

On receipt of your completed checklist and any other reference documents, I can then confirm I have a full understanding of the requirements of your sit, confirm booking and add your dates to my calendar.

YOUR NAME:

ADDRESS:

DEPARTURE
What is your expected time and date of departure?
Would you like me to be at your home prior to your departure?
If not, where will you leave the keys?

RETURN
What date and time do you expect to return?
Would you like me to be at your home on your return?
If not, what would you like me to do with keys?

Communication
Will you be contactable while away? What is your preferred contact while away?
Phone number:
Email:
Messaging: FB Messenger / Skype / Signal

PETS

What are your pet's names?
What are their meal details (times, what food, kept where, how much)?
Where do they sleep?
What exercise routines do your pets have?
What commands do your pets understand?
Favourite toys, furry friends or treats.
Do your pets have any medical problems?
Medications, schedule and method of administering.

CONTACTS

Please provide names and contact numbers of friends, family or a neighbour to contact in case of emergency:

Vet:

Pets name on file:
Do you want prior contact before taking your pet to the vet?

Electrician:

Plumber:

Cleaner:

Gardener:

Other:

Property security

Do you expect visitors for any reason? If someone needs to access your property while you're away, I need to know they have your permission. Please advise with 24hrs notice who will be visiting and for what purpose. For example, do they have permission to take something from your shed? If you know in advance that a friend or family member will be coming to your property for any reason while you are away, please list details.

Phone

Do you want me to answer the phone? If yes, what do you want me to tell callers?

Rubbish

When is rubbish and recycling collection?

Mail

Do you get mail delivery to your house? Is there a key for letterbox? Do you need mail collected from Post Office? Location? What do you want me to do with incoming mail?

GARDENS/HOUSEPLANTS

What would you like me to do with regards to watering and any other garden upkeep?

POOL/SPA

Will any maintenance need to be carried out while you are away?

WIFI / internet

Are there any bandwidth limitations to internet access?
What is the internet/WIFI password?

PARKING SPACE

Driving to sit: I require off-street parking for my vehicle (state type

and size, including height if large)
Flying to sit: I may have a rental vehicle, will discuss when confirming dates.

STORAGE SPACE

If the sit is more than two weeks, please clear some space in your fridge/freezer and pantry, and some wardrobe space in bedroom.

SEASONAL ISSUES

Summer:

Bushfire/Wildfire:
If you live in an area prone to natural fires, do you have a fire plan?
Sprinkler system to turn on?
Do you have a bag/box of important things you need me to take if evacuating property?

Cyclone/Hurricane:
If you live in the tropics, please advise me of your cyclone plan.
Do you have a safe room?
What preparation needs to be done if a cyclone warning is issued?

Water tanks/ bore water:
Are there water restrictions of any kind at your property?
Do you use tank or bore water and if so for what?

Snakes/wildlife
Do you get snakes or other wildlife on your property that may be a danger to me or your pets?
What is your usual method of minimising the danger?

Areas they are not allowed to go, or times of day they are kept locked up.

Winter:
Do you have snow in your area?
What things do I need to be aware of in regard to winter weather at your home?
Do you have a contractor clear your driveway of snow, do you have a snow blower or shovel?
Do I need to leave a tap dripping, so pipes don't freeze?
Is heating system left on low when out of the home?
Anything else . . .

General
Are there any other expectations or limitations I should be aware of?

~ ~ ~

Thank you for taking the time to complete this. It will ensure I'm aware of your expectations and are prepared for the requirements of your sit. Please return to me as soon as possible by **email** to:

Your booking can only be confirmed on my calendar when I receive your completed checklist.

Sitters' name ....

Sitters' contact details: ....

13

Reader bonuses

Discount code

The **House Sitters Group** is an international group with five websites catering to different countries. I've negotiated a **discount sign up fee** especially for readers of this book.

Australia www.aussiehousesitters.com.au
New Zealand www.kiwihousesitters.co.nz
Canada www.housesitterscanada.com
USA www.housesittersamerica.com
UK www.housesittersuk.co.uk

When you sign up as a sitter on any of their sites,
use discount code SSQ15
for a 15% discount

Community

The human need to belong is key in our search for happiness. Finding your tribe can be harder when you choose a less mainstream lifestyle, but it's also more important. Join a newsletter and community of other people who've chosen Alt Accom options, over at Stuff the Status Quo.

Acknowledgement

Writing a book is, for the most part, a solitary process. Behind every good writer and every good book, however, is a team of people who provided support, encouragement, wisdom, wine and Lindt balls.

Accountability partner - Shashi Jain. Your thoughtful questions, lateral thinking and accountability check-ins via Zoom calls between USA and Australia, were key in the early stages of getting this book out of my head and onto the pages.

Beta readers - Diane Douglas & Neil Boucher. Your honest feedback to the first draft manuscript helped me shape the book for a broader range of readers.

Travel partner - Aaron Oxwell. Our partnership over a few years of shared nomad and house sitting adventures was a blast and contributed in part to the history bank of lived experience I drew on for this book.

My Substack readers and newsletter subscribers who read and commented on early iterations of what is now a book.

Family & friends - who cheered me on, even when they don't "get" why I love the Alt Accom lifestyle so much.

ps: for future reference, my favourite Lindt balls are the white ones.

About the Author

Kellie Beckmann-Quin is an Aussie writer who enjoys finding and sharing creative solutions to issues we all face in everyday life.

She wrote her first "book" as an 8-year-old. Yep, she was the word nerd who, instead of going out to play at school recess, stayed inside and wrote stories. Back then she had one reader, her teacher.

In her 30's she published a chap book based on her blog about leaving the city to establish an island retreat. Her readers were from all over the world, and she's since met many of them in her travels.

After 25 years as a freelancer, magazine editor, news journalist and corporate communications specialist, 2024 was the year of finally writing her own stuff in her own voice again.

Her book *Stuff the Status Quo: Spend less on keeping a roof over your head and more on living a life you love*, is the first in a series exploring divergent approaches to life and living.

You can connect with me on:

🐦 https://x.com/BeckmannQuin

📘 https://www.facebook.com/beckmann.quin.7

Subscribe to newsletter:

✉ https://**stuffstatusquo**.substack.com/about

www.ingramcontent.com/pod-product-compliance
Lightning Source LLC
Chambersburg PA
CBHW060617080526
44585CB00013B/873